CW01084886

JAMES NATHAN

RECRUITING TO WIN

A TRULY COMMERCIAL INTRODUCTION TO THE WORLD OF RECRUITMENT

© James Nathan 2014 . All rights reserved

ISBN: 978-1-291-91325-5

All rights reserved. No part of this publication may be reproduced, stored in a retrieval system or transmitted in any form or by any means, electronic, mechanical, photocopying, recording or otherwise without the prior permission of the publisher.

Whilst the publisher has taken care in the preparation of this book, the publisher makes no representation, express or implied, with regard to the accuracy of the information contained in this book and cannot accept legal responsibility or liability for any errors or omissions from the book wasn't consequences thereof.

Products or services that are referred to in this book may be either trademarks and/or registered trademarks of their respective owners the publishers and authors make no claims to these trademarks.

A CIP catalogue record for this book is available from the British library.

The moral rights of the author has been asserted.

CONTENTS

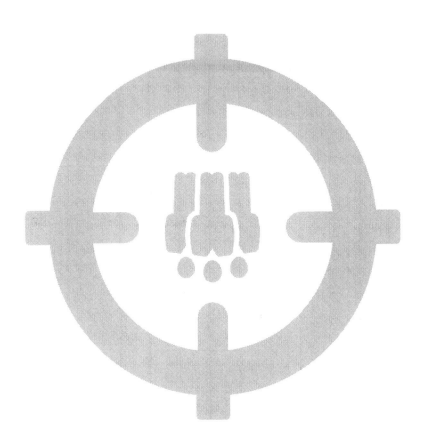

ABOUT THE AUTHOR

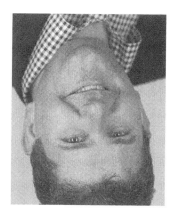

James Nathan is an enthusiastic recruitment trainer, passionate speaker and results driven coach. In addition to being an author, he is the founder of the jne Recruitment Academy and its eLearning counterpart Impact Recruitment Training; training businesses designed to unlock and grow the natural potential of people in recruiting roles.

James is one of the UK's most experienced and successful Professional Recruitment Trainers, with over 16 years experience in helping people within the profession learn and grow their sales and business development skills.

James specialises in working with both people who are new to a recruitment environment and helping them to learn the basic skills on which to build a broader career, as well as with those with solid experience to grow and develop their skills further and then really take off.

Before setting up his own recruitment business, James spent nearly 12 years of his career with a multi-national recruitment group, where he built and ran a network of Regional and London offices as well as leading on training and development programmes in both the Finance and Legal businesses.

"THE BEST RECRUITERS WEREN'T BORN WITH SOME SPECIAL TALENT. THEY WERE TRAINED, COACHED AND MENTORED. AND, ANYONE CAN JOIN THEM."

INTRODUCTION

The world of recruitment is a truly fantastic place and one in which it is very possible to build a wonderful and long term career.

My story is very similar to many others. Shortly after qualifying as an accountant, I looked to leave the profession and considered my options. I loved the business side of accountancy and the interaction with clients, but didn't see myself as a Partner, and wondered what else the world outside offered. In-house Accountancy? No, too similar. Something completely different? Definitely. I needed somewhere to use my commercial background and business skills, but somewhere I could be myself, learn and grow. Somewhere I could be rewarded for hard work, and build a great career.

I happily discovered recruitment (a little by accident as many in those days did), but I like to think that recruitment found me, and it was love at first cold call.

Things have happily moved on a long way since then. Not only is the technology a world further on, but we also have a profession in which people actively seek a career rather than happen upon it. Recruitment is now regularly a first choice for university graduates, and a sensible alternative to anyone looking to build a career outside of their initial chosen profession. Long may this continue.

I have been really fortunate in my career to have been trained, mentored and guided by some of the most intelligent, dynamic and influential characters in the profession. People who cared deeply about their directors, managers and consultants, people who put all the effort they could into developing their staff, regardless of level, to be the best they could be.

Since having focused my career in business development and recruitment sales training, I have come to appreciate just how rare these kinds of managers are. So often I am astounded at the real lack of training and guidance made available to new consultants. So many are still shown a desk and told to get on with it, and in return a large number of potentially great consultants leave the profession dissolutioned.

I want to help change this. I want everyone entering the profession to get the best possible real world training and advice available. The kind of training I received, and have tried to give to everyone I have trained since.

I know that not every recruitment business can afford to hire in-house trainers, and the alternative - sending staff away from the office for off-site training, (with potentially a classroom full of competitor staff) may not be what you are looking for.

Whether you are a sole trader, a small business or working in a very large company, this book is designed to fill the gap.

WHO IS THIS BOOK FOR

I have written this book to be simple, plain speaking and accessible to anyone looking to improve their recruitment, commercial and sales skills within the recruitment industry.

You may be reading this for yourself as an introduction, using it as a refresher, or perhaps looking to refocus and improve your skills. Similarly you may be using it as step-by-step guide for new consultants in your team, to be worked through in conjunction with your in-house or on the desk training.

Most importantly this book is written to be a commercially focused and practical guide for professional recruiters. It teaches real world recruitment, something other guides often forget to do.

Recruitment is a sales business, plain and simple. Our job is to make profit by placing people into new roles and helping our clients find the best staff. Of course we help people in the process, but at its core, recruitment is fundamentally commercial.

 I HAVE WRITTEN THIS BOOK TO BE SIMPLE, PLAIN SPEAKING AND ACCESSIBLE TO ANYONE LOOKING TO IMPROVE THEIR RECRUITMENT, COMMERCIAL AND SALES SKILLS WITHIN THE RECRUITMENT INDUSTRY."

HOW TO USE THIS BOOK

The text is organised into ten logical chapters in which you will find a mixture of learning content, action points, top tips, things to note and remember, and points specific to the temps market.

Action points, top tips, things to note and remember and 'Think Temps' are highlighted in the margins.

The temps reminders ('Think Temps') are added to help both temps and permanent consultants understand the differences in markets, as well as the opportunities to upsell and cross-sell, adding both value and profit.

This book is written not only to be read cover to cover, but also to be skimmed, studied and returned to as time goes by.

Learning the basic of recruitment is absolutely vital to your career going forward. Recruiting to Win will teach you every thing you need to know, to really get going on the path to great success.

Enjoy and all the best of luck!

CHAPTER 1 – THE RECRUITMENT INDUSTRY

H ello, and welcome to the first chapter in your journey into the fantastic world of recruitment. In this chapter, we are going to look at:

- the recruitment industry,

- how it's made up,

- how people recruit,

- the difference between executive search, professional recruitment and generalist staffing.

INDUSTRY OVERVIEW

The recruitment industry is a constantly changing and growing market sector, making it a fantastic industry in which to build an exciting and commercially fulfilling career.

The recruitment sector - some facts

- There are over 91,000 people currently working in recruitment in the UK, a 13% increase year on year, and numbers are only set to increase.

- The sector is heavily affected by movements in the global economy. There has been huge change across the past few years as the general economy moves out of recession, with turnover volumes only recently returning to pre 2006/2007 levels.

- The global recruitment market is currently estimated to be worth in excess of £100b, with the UK accounting for around £26.5b (2013), split roughly between £24b temporary, and £2.5b permanent.

- Forecasts predict the industry's annual growth at 7.3% this financial year (2014/15), a step increase from 4.7% in 2012/13. This represents a potential industry turnover peak in 2014/15 of £30b.

Sources: rec.uk.com and Skipton Business Finance 2014

The global recruitment market is roughly split into 3 categories:

The professional recruitment market

The industry has seen its greatest growth in the professional marketplace, allowing specialist recruiters in this market niche to grow ahead of the overall recruitment market. This growth has been characterised by:

- Increased outsourcing, fuelled by shortages of high quality candidates and higher skills at a premium

- Dynamic growth in the service and technology sectors

- Increased workforce mobility

- A growth in truly international organisations and careers

- Increases in specialism, focused on industry, geography and discipline.

EXECUTIVE SEARCH

Often known as 'headhunting', executive search is a recruitment methodology typically used for senior-level jobs, for which there is a smaller pool of appropriate, high-level candidates who can be identified and targeted.

Search is proactive, targeting candidates for a specific role. These candidates may or may not be looking for a job move.

The Search Process

The process involves the client paying a retainer fee to the search firm, who then identify a pool of potentially relevant candidates (the long list). From this list, a more specific list is decided upon, and candidates approached. If they are interested, the consultant would then interview them (pre-screening).

The consultant will produce a short list from these interviews which will be provided to the client. The client will then perform their own interview process, and a successful candidate offered the role.

Roles are typically permanent, although in recent years, a number of search firms have begun to work on higher level temporary roles, known as interim assignments. These include projects, maternity cover, sickness cover and handover periods.

The search process can be lengthy and requires the client to pay fees on a scheduled basis. Usually this means a 'retainer fee' of 1/3 of the total fee agreed, a 'shortlist fee' (1/3) on production of a shortlist, and a 'completion fee' (the final 1/3) on an offer being made or acceptance achieved. In some cases, the fees are payable in monthly instalments from the point where an assignment is started, and is payable regardless of whether a candidate is recruited or not.

Alternatives to Search include:
Advertised Selection – where the recruiter utilises an advertising medium to attract candidates (on or offline). The consultant will then pre-screen the candidates and provide a shortlist to the client.

Hybrid Selection – where both search and advertising are used simultaneously to provide a shortlist.

The Search Market
The Search market is characterised by a large number of privately owned firms. Typically these operate by sector specialism, and then by discipline (sometimes known as vertical markets).

True Search is a very specialist process, and fees charged tend to be in the range of 30 to 35% of a candidate's starting package.

Search firms maintain a limited database, and employ researchers to identify candidates and produce market maps (a document outlining where the potential candidates for a role are currently working). Search firms also tend to have a more limited client base than other types of recruitment businesses and maintain 'off limits' clients (clients that they may not headhunt from).

PROFESSIONAL RECRUITMENT

Sometimes known as the mid-market, professional recruitment is used for a wide variety of roles, from junior to very senior. Fees for this style of recruitment tend to be contingent, which means that a fee is only charged when a placement is made.

In most cases, a continent recruiter will hold an extensive database of candidates, who are looking for a career move. They will use this database to identify an appropriate shortlist of candidates, which is then shown to a client.

Roles may be either permanent or temporary, or a combination of both.

Methodologies Used

Professional recruiters may use a variety of methodologies, including advertised selection, search and database selection. Although the majority of roles worked on are on a contingent basis, the recruiter may also be retained on an assignment. A retained assignment is one in which the client pays a proportion of the final fee upfront (a retainer fee) and then a proportion on shortlist and at completion.

Roles can be worked on exclusively, i.e. as a sole supplier to the client, or in competition with one or more other recruitment providers.

Retained assignments are discussed in more detail in a later module.

The Professional Recruitment Market

The mid-market is typified by a large number of companies ranging from small boutique businesses to international recruitment brands, with sector specialism and expertise. Roles recruited may range from graduate level, through middle management, to senior executive.

Fees tend to be in the range of 20 to 30% of starting salary, although these may vary depending on the volume of recruitment, preferred supplier agreements, market conditions and level of exclusivity gained.

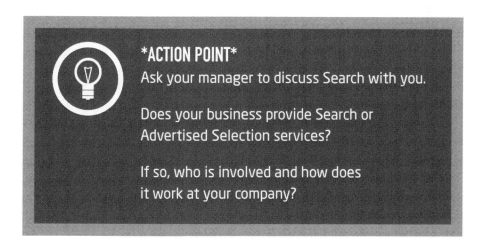

ACTION POINT
Ask your manager to discuss Search with you.

Does your business provide Search or Advertised Selection services?

If so, who is involved and how does it work at your company?

GENERALIST STAFFING

This segment of the recruitment market covers more junior roles, clerical roles, or trade style roles and may include some graduate recruitment.

It is a fiercely competitive market sector, characterised by high volumes and lower fees. Most recruitment is on a contingent basis, although some large scale contracts or assignments may involve a retained element.

Generalist staffing involves a quick turnaround on assignments, working with actively registered candidates, and clients tend to use a number of agents to source vacancies at any one time rather then relying on exclusive relationships.

Roles may be permanent or temporary.

The Generalist Market

This market place is dominated by large international recruitment companies, and fees tend to be in the 10 to 20% range. This will vary massively depending on role level, volume of recruitment and preferred supplier status.

CHAPTER 2 – CANDIDATE MANAGEMENT

Looking after our candidates is just as important to a recruitment business as looking after clients. This is because they are in fact the same thing!

A person may be a client, using us to find staff for his/her business one minute, and a candidate, looking for a career move for themselves the next. Or even at the same time!

High quality candidate management is vital, and building strong relationships with our candidates will pay enormous dividends later on.

A junior candidate who is very well looked after and given our very best service today, is highly likely to remember us in the future, and use us to recruit all their staff when they are Managing Director of a huge company!

> HIGH QUALITY CANDIDATE MANAGEMENT IS VITAL, AND BUILDING STRONG RELATIONSHIPS WITH OUR CANDIDATES WILL PAY ENORMOUS DIVIDENDS LATER ON.

In this chapter, we will look at:

- The candidate cycle,

- Candidate sourcing,

- Registration

- Updating.

Candidate interviewing is dealt with in the next chapter.

THE CANDIDATE CYCLE

The candidate cycle (shown in the diagram opposite) is in essence the life-cycle of a candidate from their first contract with us – whether that is by telephone, email or drop in, through updating, selling them roles, managing the interview process, offer management and aftercare.

Ideally, this process should be of such high quality and service that the candidate becomes our client in their new role.

 THE CANDIDATE CYCLE (SHOWN IN THE DIAGRAM OPPOSITE) IS IN ESSENCE THE LIFE-CYCLE OF A CANDIDATE FROM THEIR FIRST CONTRACT WITH US.

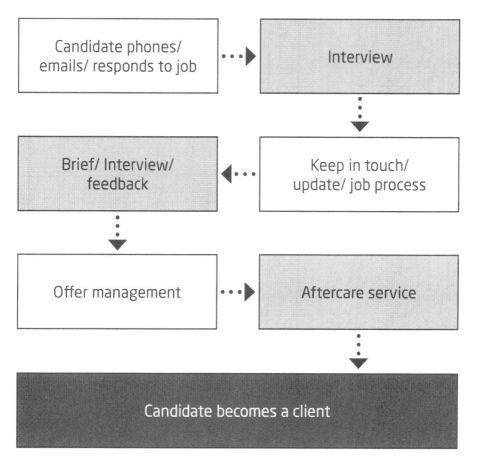

In this module we are going to cover the first part of the candidate cycle. The remaining parts will be dealt with in the jobs and interview/ offer management modules.

SOURCING CANDIDATES

Sourcing quality candidates is vital to the long term survival and growth of recruitment businesses. Without them, you won't be able to provide your clients with the best and right people at all times. This is particularly important in candidate driven markets – i.e. markets where there are many available jobs, but few available candidates.

Where do candidates come from?
There are many ways that recruitment businesses get the candidates they then sell on to their clients. Here is a selection of the main ones:

- **Search/Headhunting**

- **Advertising (off-line)** – These can be either general or client paid – national press, trade press, local press, direct mail

- **On-line advertising** – Your own business's website but can also include accumulator web-sites e.g. Total Jobs, Monster, Job-site, etc

- **Personal referrals** *

- **Referrals from other offices or divisions in your business**

- **Candidate entertainment events** – including professional student groups and graduate events

- **Seminars**

- **Clients becoming candidates**

- **General registrations from your company's branding and profile**

* Personal Referrals - By far the best, most effective and cheapest medium of sourcing candidates is by personal referral. The better you serve your client and candidates, the better your referral rates will be. Getting personal referrals requires:

- A professional and consistent approach

- Excellent candidate care

- Consultative advice

- Face to face working

- You must ask!

Opportunities to ask for referrals include:

- When selling a role to a registered candidate and they are not interested, ask if they know anyone who might be.

- At interview, if you have built a good level of rapport, ask the candidate if they have any friends or colleagues you might be introduced to. Give them some of your business cards to hand out.

- At registration - over the phone.

- On a successful placement. Take the candidate for a celebratory drink or meal and ask for referrals. If you have done a great job for them they should be very receptive.

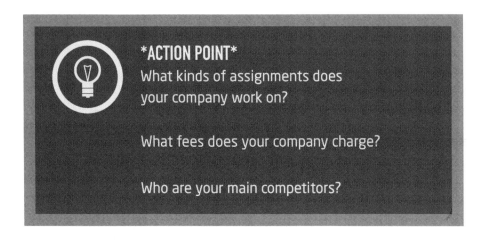

ACTION POINT
What kinds of assignments does
your company work on?

What fees does your company charge?

Who are your main competitors?

REGISTRATION

When we register a candidate, our key objective is to improve the quality, efficiency and effectiveness of registration, and thereby increase the likelihood of obtaining exclusivity from the outset.

The two main methods of registration are
1. Via the telephone
2. Face to face

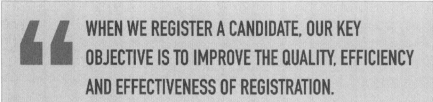

WHEN WE REGISTER A CANDIDATE, OUR KEY OBJECTIVE IS TO IMPROVE THE QUALITY, EFFICIENCY AND EFFECTIVENESS OF REGISTRATION.

Candidates may also show up at the office (often known as a 'walk-in'), but this is less common.

Which approach we choose will be decided by:

- Time pressure – ours and theirs

- Whether they fit an immediate job vacancy we have

- How 'good' a candidate we think they are

ACTION POINT
To help with the initial conversation – why not build yourself a Telephone Enquiry Form (TNQ) that relates specifically to your market and industry.

Talk with your manager about what this should include.

Advantages and Disadvantages of Each Approach

Telephone - quicker but more difficult to build rapport.

Face to Face - easier to sum up a candidate in order to sell them as well as easier to build rapport but time consuming.

THINK TEMPS!

Telephone registrations are imperative for Temps due to the volume and speed required. It is particularly critical to obtain all relevant information and decide immediately on a candidate's suitability. 5 to 10 minutes spent taking a good TNQ will save 30 to 60 minutes if the wrong candidate is invited for interview.

Key Information Required

- Name

- Address and contact phone numbers

- Current/most recent position and employer

- Current/most recent responsibilities

- Qualifications (professional and academic)

- Exam record (if part qualified)

- Is CV available/up to date?

- Reason for looking

- Broadly what they are looking for (sector, salary role, location etc)

- Specialist Skills (especially important for Temps)

- Previous contact with our business

- Current/last salary

- Required salary

- Temp or Perm? Both?

- How did they hear of us?

- Who else are they registered with? (competitors)

What We Need To Do

We must make sure that we are making the most of this initial conversation, to gain control and ideally, exclusivity. We need to keep the following in mind, and where possible:

- Agree actions - them sending in a CV, booking them in for interview, accept or reject on an advertisement

- Agree the appropriate consultant to look after them (point of contact)

- Agree timetable for them

- Obtain exclusivity - where appropriate and feasible

- Offer advice and comment - which will help get their buy-in

- Probe for leads - where else are they interviewing, what other jobs are they being told about etc

- Ask for referrals of other candidates - their friends and colleagues

- Record all the information that we get onto our database

Critical Success Factors

Here are some further things to keep in mind for a highly successful outcome:

- Always keep a positive attitude and approach

- Be polite

- Use good listening skills and probing questions

- Have empathy

- Sound interested

- Be enthusiastic

- Be professional

- Be knowledgeable

- Ask open questions - who, which, why, where, when and how

- Take the necessary amount of time

- Maintain attention to detail

REMEMBER
Effective registration is key to
any recruitment business

- First impressions count and can remain for many years

- It wastes time later if adequate information is not taken
  at the start

- The correct approach can ensure exclusivity

- Ineffective registrations can result in missed revenue
  or placements!

CANDIDATE UPDATING

Why bother to update?

Keeping in touch with candidates is a vital part of the recruitment
process. The advantages of keeping up to date are numerous, and here
are some key ones:

- **Saves us time** - maintains the size of our database, avoids
  briefing candidates about irrelevant roles,

- **Maintains contact** with the candidate

- **Builds rapport** *, trust and loyalty - this means we have greater control

- Lets us check **if the candidates, situation, parameters or expectations have changed**

- Allows us to **pick up leads** *

- Provides **competitor information**

- **Identifies potential recruitment consultants** to headhunt for our own business

- Provides **understanding about the company** they work for and what is happening there

- To gain **recommendations and personal referrals** *

* THE MOST KEY ADVANTAGES

How often should we update?
How often we keep in touch with candidates to update will depend on the market that you are working in and how 'key/hot' a candidate is. Whether a candidate is considered key/hot is determined by their place-ability in your individual market. Your manager will be able to discuss this with you.

The following is a good guide for updating, if your manager doesn't have a specific guideline that he/she would like you to work to.

Temporary Candidates:	Once a week (monthly if on long term contract)
Key/Hot Permanent Candidates:	Every 30 days minimum
Non-Key Permanent Candidates:	Every 90 days minimum

ACTION POINT

Talk with your manager about what is the norm in your business.

How many candidates are you responsible for?

How often are you expected to contact them?

CHAPTER 3 – CANDIDATE INTERVIEWING

M eeting and interviewing a candidate is a vital part of the registration process. It is a great opportunity to build a relationship with the candidate, build rapport, build understanding and gain information and leads about the candidate's business, market place and market knowledge.

In this chapter we will look at:

- Interview structure,

- Potential difficulties,

- Additional information needed and

- Gaining candidate exclusivity.

INTERVIEW STRUCTURE

Candidate interviews are ultimately a dual purpose process:

1. What you need to know and learn about a candidate to help (sell) them, and

2. What business information you can gather for your own business needs.

Although best done face-to-face, where time is very short it may be necessary to interview by telephone. If this is the case, the process should be followed by telephone in the same way.

All interviews should follow a clear structure. This is outlined below:

Introduction

It is important to start the interview in a way which starts to build rapport, but also puts the candidate at ease.

 WHEN WE REGISTER A CANDIDATE, OUR KEY OBJECTIVE IS TO IMPROVE THE QUALITY, EFFICIENCY AND EFFECTIVENESS OF REGISTRATION.

IMPORTANT NOTE
Don't forget that candidates may be very
nervous, or anxious about meeting you.

Moving jobs isn't something that people choose
to do lightly, and there may be a mixture of
emotions at play.

Similarly, if the person you are meeting
has just been made redundant,
they may not be at their best!

- Start by introducing yourself, passing pleasantries and
  breaking the ice - e.g. "how was your journey?", "did you find us
  okay?", "have you been to this building before?"

- Set the agenda for the meeting, in a soft way e.g. "What I
  would like to do is talk about you and your experience, then
  discuss why it is that you are looking, and what you are looking
  for next. Then, perhaps we can discuss what the market is like,
  and how we can help you. Is that okay?"

This will give the candidate a framework, whilst allowing you to
remain in control of the structure - very important.

- You are looking to create a highly credible impression: friendly
  and professional, mature, relaxed and sensible.

TOP TIPS
In any meeting, the person asking the questions is in control and the person answering them is being led.

You must maintain rapport, whilst remaining in control.

Ask a question and listen to the answer, before asking the next question

You have two ears and one mouth - use them in that proportion

Core of the Interview

Before the interview it is really important that you take the time to read the candidate's CV and do any internet research you can about them, e.g. LinkedIn and company web sites.

From this preparation you will be aware of anything missing, e.g. date of birth, telephone numbers, gaps in experience etc.

- Talk through their experience in chronological order, starting with early career

- When discussing each job, find out about the following before moving on (but remember to use your judgment, especially when dealing with more senior candidates:

- o   The company and what they do
- o   The structure and size of the department *
- o   Who they reported to *
- o   What they learned or gained in the role
- o   Why they joined the business and why they left

* This information is very important for business development - see later module.

- Ensure that you find out what the individual actually did/does in the role, and the scope of their responsibilities - this may also require an understanding of what percentage of their time was spent on those tasks

- Find out their strengths and weaknesses, as well as what they can and cannot do

- Understand why they are looking to move from their current role - it is imperative to cover this in some detail, and understand their reasoning (this will also help to 'close' them later on in offer management).

- Ascertain the type of role they are looking for and why. Advise on the reality/likelihood of them achieving this.

- What is their current salary and package - and what their expectations are in the next role. Advise on this.

- Find out what they have done so far in their job search. Which other consultants are they registered with? Who do they rate?

- What other interviews have they been to, or roles have they had discussed with them? (LEADS!)

REMEMBER
If the candidate is really good/placeable (sometimes referred to as 'hot') - you must try to gain exclusivity or prevent them registering with more agencies.

More on exclusivity later in this chapter.

Conclusion

- Explain how your business works and what they can expect
  - e.g. that other consultants from your business may contact them, that you will be the main point of contact etc

Remember
We are looking to ensure that we manage their expectations, whilst maintaining their respect and faith in our professionalism

Ask if they have any questions

- Conclude with an ACTION PLAN. (All action plans should summarise the interview and what we and they are going to do. The best way to do this is to follow the following summary, and repeat back to them)

ROLE: What they are looking for

SIZE: Size of business they are looking to join: small, large, indifferent

SECTOR: Public, Private, Industry etc

RFL: Reason for Leaving/Looking?

SALARY: Review expectations

OTHER: What else have they done?

BUYBACK: What will happen if/when they resign
Will they need advice in how to deal with a buy back
i.e. where the company tries to keep them

CONCLUDE: What we are going to do now is....

THINK TEMPS

When interviewing someone for temporary work, you need to get a very good idea of their saleable skills. Many people will do less important or interesting roles for short term contracts, at a rate below what they might want in the permanent market.

Make sure you manage expectations heavily and be sure to sell the advantages of temporary/contract work.

POTENTIAL DIFFICULTIES IN THE INTERVIEW

Here are a few ideas of things that typically lead to problems or difficulties in a candidate interview, as well as some skills and actions to overcome them.

TOP TIPS
The more practicing you do and the more candidates you meet, the better you will become at interviewing

Potential difficulties

- Poor planning leading to an unclear structure

- Consultant talks too much

- Monosyllabic or uncommunicative candidates

- Hooks/leads are missing or not explored

- Not probing enough or challenging/stretching the candidate enough

- Interview takes too long (or interview not long enough)

- Failure to agree a reasonable action plan

- Market information not ascertained

- Failure to consider the candidate as a consultant to work with your business

- Too many closed questions

- Too much (or too little) rapport

- Lack of confidence with senior/imposing candidates

- Candidates' preconceived ideas (the interview is a great opportunity to challenge these)

- Overly formal (or too informal)

Skills/Actions to overcome potential difficulties

- Set the agenda (i.e. structure) at the beginning of the interview

- Read the CV first!

- Ask open questions (how, what, when, where, which, who)

- Prepare, prepare, prepare

- Time management

- Summarising

- Listening - actively (2 ears, one mouth)

- Varying the balance of control and rapport

- Consultative selling

- Use of silence

- 80% candidate talks, 20% consultant talks

- Identification of key information

- A professional impression

- Ability to advise, control and manage expectations (up or down)

ADDITIONAL INFORMATION NEEDED

What other information do we need? (In addition to registration details)

Once we have gained the hard and fast information needed, there are some softer details that are useful for us to understand.

Here are some to start with, but what others can you think of?

- Any ties or constraints on location

- Personal motivations/real needs

- The type of culture preferred

- Family related requirements, e.g. flexibility for school pick-ups etc

And then there are a few other things that we would like to know for our business:

- Competitor information or activity

- Market information – e.g. how did they get their current role etc

- Would they be a good consultant for us? Why sell a candidate for £x when they could bill £xxx working with us!

In summary, what should the interview achieve?

- A credible impression

- Rapport

- Trust (nothing happens without trust!)

- Control of the process

- Understanding the personality and motivations of the candidate

- Identification of the candidates saleable skills

- An action plan/timetable

- Captured the candidate's interest

- Managed the candidate's expectations

- Advised the candidate of the available options (including temp/ perm or other divisions of our business)

REMEMBER
If we do this right, then there is a much greater likelihood of the candidate referring their friends and colleagues to us, as well as using us when they become a client in the future.

ACTION POINT
Sit in on as many candidate interviews as you can with more experienced consultants. This will allow you to learn different styles and approaches to interviewing.

Interview as many candidates as you can. The more you do, the better and more natural you will become.

Practice makes perfect!

GAINING EXCLUSIVITY

Commercially it is very important that we keep the best candidates exclusive to us. This stops our competitors placing them (especially with our clients).

Trust and respect are everything

In order to gain exclusivity, you will need to gain the trust and respect of the candidate, as well as the understanding that you have the market covered for them. If you get this right, then they won't feel the need to register with other agents.

Initially in the candidate interview you will have asked them who else they are registered with. If the answer is none, or none yet, then a simple "are you happy to leave it with just me?" should do the trick.

If you have gained their trust and respect, the answer is usually yes.

However, if the candidate is keen to register with other agents, then you will need to sell the benefits of sole registration. Examples include:

- You are unlikely to miss any roles through us, as the majority of businesses would use us to recruit

- We can guarantee control of your CV, in that it will not go out to a client without your express permission, to ensure confidentiality

If they are already registered elsewhere, try to limit any further registrations.

WARNING!
DO NOT sell exclusivity to a candidate you feel will be difficult to help. The candidate will be solely reliant on you and you will be unlikely to fulfil your promise to them. This will only result in an unhappy candidate, and a future unhappy client who is unlikely to use you or your business to recruit in the future.

IMPORTANT NOTE
A candidate's expectations must always be effectively managed.

People value honesty, and under-delivery is worse than telling them that you can't help in the first place!

CHAPTER 4 – THE CV (RÉSUMÉ)

The Curriculum Vitae (CV) is a particularly important document:

- It is often the first contact between Client and Candidate, and

- It reflects both the quality of a candidate
  and your professionalism.

In this chapter we will look at:

- What is a good CV,

- What employers are looking for in a CV, and

- CV dos and don'ts.

A GOOD CV

A good CV can be the difference between securing an interview or not, by hooking the reader's attention and selling the candidate well.

A CV is a marketing document, and should be treated as such. You must take the time to ensure that the CVs you use are the best they can be. A few extra minutes taken here can make all the difference.

REMEMBER
Internal recruiters and hiring managers can receive literally hundreds of CVs, and only have time to scan them at best.Your candidate's CVs need to make an impact.

A good CV will need to communicate the relevant information in a clear, concise and easily readable form.

It is the candidate's CV

Where ever possible, the candidate themselves should write their own CV. This will ensure that the onus is on them to for it to be factually accurate. However, you may need to guide the candidate to help them provide you with the necessary information relevant to a role.

In the next section we will look at what a client is looking for in a CV.

ACTION POINT
Does your business use a standard
format for CVs?

Or do you just use the CV as the candidate
sends it to you?

What employers look for in a CV

The CVs that you show your clients must be written to give the very best chance of securing a first interview. They are the first foot in the door.

Your candidate might be a great fit for a role, but unless the CV shows that, there is little chance of agreeing an interview for them.

Although it may be tempting to use a generic CV for all the roles that you put a candidate forward to, a tailored and specific CV will give you a far better chance of success.

YOUR CANDIDATE MIGHT BE A GREAT FIT FOR A ROLE, BUT UNLESS THE CV SHOWS THAT, THERE IS LITTLE CHANCE OF AGREEING AN INTERVIEW FOR THEM.

TOP TIPS

The person doing the first sift of CVs is rarely the ultimate decision maker.

Making the CV stand out by showing experience specific to a particular role makes it much easier for that person to put your CVs in the 'yes' pile!

CV Impact

For your CVs to have an impact with clients they should show the following information in a succinct and easy to read format:

Roles and responsibilities: These should be tailored to the specific vacancy, and the job titles and information used must be relevant.

Experience: This should be consistent and relevant to the specific vacancy. It should show where the candidate adds value and how they contribute to the business.

Skills: All relevant skills should be included and these will complement the experience shown. They should illustrate suitability to a role.

Achievements: People love overachievers. Make sure that where ever possible, how a candidate has beaten targets, added profit, and made achievements, are shown clearly.

Education: Make sure that relevant education and professional qualifications are listed, particularly if these are listed as required or desirable on a job spec.

Once you have the details required, then the CV will need to read well as a whole document, and be sure to grab the reader's attention.

It should be:

- **VERY easy to read** - a nice, clear and consistent format. Use bullet points to highlight relevant skills and experience etc.

- **Consistent** - in chronological order, no unexplained gaps or inconsistencies.

- **Relevant** - use language that fits the job spec and makes keywords instantly recognisable.

- **Easy to open** - use a widely used format, e.g. MS Word, or PDF. Make life as easy as possible for the reader.

CV dos and don'ts

As we know, an employer may spend less than 30 seconds making a decision over each CV that they read.

Here are a list of things to avoid, to help you get your CVs put into the 'yes' pile:

Don't use photos or fancy fonts - the best CV, not the nicest picture or font wins the interview

Do use a clear, clean format, that is easy to read

Don't use clichés and buzzwords - 'team player', 'motivated', 'dynamic', 'results driven' etc etc, should be avoided

Do make the candidate's relevant experience clear and easy to understand

Don't use jargon - assume the reader has no understanding of the candidate's business

Do make sure your CVs are spell checked and free from errors

Do keep it brief - no more than 2 to 3 pages

Don't include irrelevant personal details such as age, religion and sex

Do bullet point

Don't include reasons for leaving roles (although the candidate must be able to answer these in an interview)

DON'T USE CLICHÉS AND BUZZWORDS — 'TEAM PLAYER', 'MOTIVATED', 'DYNAMIC', 'RESULTS DRIVEN' ETC ETC, SHOULD BE AVOIDED.

CHAPTER 5 – INTRODUCTION TO BUSINESS DEVELOPMENT

An introduction to the great art of BD

Business development is a vital part of what we do as recruitment consultants. Unfortunately, it is the part of the job that many people have a mental block with, and many others treat as a chore. But, it really shouldn't be that way.

BD (as it is usually called) can be one of the most rewarding parts of what you do. Building relationships with new contacts and winning their business, as well as building stronger relationships with existing clients to become preferred suppliers are the things that make the difference between an average job filler, and a real business builder.

Some people call BD cold calling. But, phoning people is only a small part of what we do.

In this chapter we will look at:

- Why people buy

- Features Vs Benefits, and

- The business development process

Why people buy

People buy things for many reasons. In order to sell well we need to really understand the individual person we are working with. We need to ask questions, and build a strong understanding so that we can provide them with the right solution.

Much is written around this subject, but for simplicity I am going to break it down into some small chunks.

Why we buy anything

- We actually have a need for it

- We perceive that it offers value for money

- We have convinced ourselves that we need it

- People like to buy things

- Because we like the salesperson!

People buy things and especially expensive things because they perceive value. Think for a minute about why someone would buy a Rolex watch for £5000 when a Casio would do the same basic job for a lot less!

We are unlikely to buy something unless we have convinced ourselves that we need it. The key to any sales, is therefore, the motivation to buy.

TOP TIPS
People buy people
They buy you before they buy from you

The days of pushy sales are well and truly
over. No one likes to be sold to, but everybody
likes to buy

Consider for a moment how you would respond to the following:

- A cold call being read from a script

- A pushy salesperson who doesn't consider your needs

- A salesperson not listening to you

- Being offered a product that you don't really want, even though it is well priced

- A salesperson who listens, not saying much, but somehow gets you to open up

FEATURES VS BENEFITS

It is really important that at this stage of your career you really understand the difference between Features and Benefits.

It is a critical concept, and one that if understood now will stand you in very good stead in the future.

A **Feature** is a factual statement about a product or service. Features are NOT what entice a client to buy.

A **Benefit** answers the question "what's in it for me?" - meaning that the product provides the client with something of value to them. It focuses on results. This is where most people go wrong; they often just elaborate on the feature.

The **Real Benefit** is the key.

Here's a simple example

Feature: Anti locking brakes (ABS) on a new car

Benefit: Increased Safety (but this is not the real benefit!)

Real Benefit: We will all be okay if I have to brake hard with my family in the car. I will be more confident driving in bad weather.

To sell your client the **Real Benefits** of your solution you need to:

1. Really know your client

2. View things from your client's perspective

Viewing things from your own perspective means that you automatically fill in any gaps with assumptions. You must put yourself in your client's shoes and approach the solution as if you have never seen it before. Then ask "What's in it for me?"

3. Think in terms of results

If you think in terms of Features Vs Results the situation will become even clearer. Ask "What results will I get from this feature?" If you do you will be sure that your message will be right on the mark.

ACTION POINT
Talk to your manager about the Features Vs Benefits of your services.

Identify several features e.g. interviewing candidates before putting them forward to jobs, and then identify the real benefits to a client.

Think about how you will describe the benefits of a solution next time.

More thoughts
We often think of Benefits in terms of clients. When thinking "What's in it for me?" you need to think about:

- **Benefits to the client**
- **Benefits to the candidate**
- **Benefits to you!**

BD PROCESS

Where do we start?

Focus and preparation are the keys to success. BD should not be a random process that is fitted in when possible.

BD should be a considered and planned process which acts as an undercurrent to everything that you do. A good BD process can make the difference between getting the odd job in and filling it, and having a continual stream of roles and positions to work on, and meetings to attend.

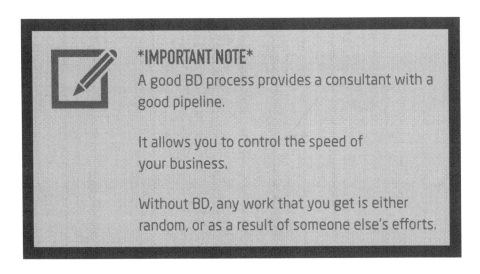

IMPORTANT NOTE
A good BD process provides a consultant with a good pipeline.

It allows you to control the speed of your business.

Without BD, any work that you get is either random, or as a result of someone else's efforts.

Prioritisation

Imagine for a moment that you have been given responsibility for an office. Here are some questions you should ask yourself about your client base in order to help you prioritise:

- Who are our key clients?

- Who are the decision makers in those clients?

- How much business do we transact?

- Where are we missing revenue? i.e. where are our competitors making money?

- Where have we missed revenue in the past?

- How frequently are they being contacted? (if at all)

- Are we networking? Do we know all the relevant contacts, including contacts who are 'temp' contacts?

- Which companies are growing in or moving to our area?

- Can we afford to forget the non-key clients

- Can we cross-sell or upsell?

Planning our BD

We need to develop a methodology and structure around each activity involving our clients.

Great habits to get into include:

- Use a daily, weekly and monthly plan – particularly when planning the calls you want to make

- Work on one large client at a time, rather than a scatter gun approach; you will learn more and get better results

- Diarise calls and follow ups in your diary or on your database/Customer Relationship Management (CRM) system

- Be rigorous about this

TOP TIPS
Never forget the personal touch.

Talk to your colleagues about your clients and their experiences and history of dealing with them.

Consultants may not have recorded as much information onto your system as might be helpful!

CHAPTER 6 – TELEPHONE TECHNIQUES

The telephone is one of our most important tools in BD. We can use it for building new relationships and we can use it for developing existing relationships.

In this chapter we will look at:

- Phone vs email, and

- Three of the most important techniques to master early in your career:

    1. **Introductory calling**
    2. **Ad-chasing, and**
    3. **Lead chasing**

PHONE VS EMAIL IN BD

The phone allows for two-way communication, and this is really important. With the advent of email, much of what really should be done by telephone, is instead often done by email. Email is great for some things, but it doesn't allow for two-way communication. You cannot build a relationship by typing.

When we speak with people we can ask questions and respond to what they say. We can use our voice tone, volume and style to build rapport. We can probe and delve. New information can be gained. We can control and persuade.

It is also much harder to ignore someone speaking with you, and you can't just delete them!

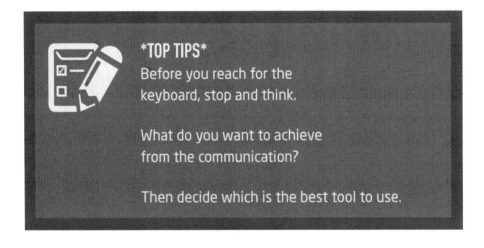

TOP TIPS
Before you reach for the keyboard, stop and think.

What do you want to achieve from the communication?

Then decide which is the best tool to use.

MAKING INTRODUCTORY CALLS

This is NOT Cold Calling

Cold calling is an awful term for these introductory calls, and can in itself put people off. If we re-phrase this and call it introductory calling, it is already a little easier to face up to. If we take things further and think about making calls to people we know, have met or have a connection with, then it becomes warm calling.

If the call is a follow up as a result of having met someone at an event, or been linked with them on social media (particularly LinkedIn) then it's easier still.

I am not going to kid you into thinking that you are going to instantly feel comfortable making these calls. You are not, you might be a little nervous and you are going to make mistakes. But then again, have you ever done something new perfectly the first time? I certainly haven't. What I can promise you is that with practice you will get better, your comfort level will increase and you will start to get results more quickly.

Top tips for making introduction calls

- Make time in your diary to plan your calling

- Block off time in your diary to make the calls (10am is a great time)

- Decide who you want to speak with and make a provisional list

- Do some research into your potential contacts so that you feel well prepared

- Plan your introduction and some questions for the call

- Set yourself a minimum and maximum objective for the call

- Take some time to practice

- Think about how good you will feel when you have got your first meeting with a potential client

- Make the calls

- Reap the rewards!

IMPORTANT NOTE

This is very important; don't call your most important potential client first.

Start by making a number of calls to people who don't matter as much.

I know you are going to say that all people matter, but in terms of learning to call well, you need to make the first calls to those who you can bear not to get work from.

Once you are comfortable and have built a style, then call the more important people.

Don't put it off
Whatever you do, don't look at your list, and make excuses not to call them. The person you don't call is without doubt the person who is just about to hire someone with your skills, or knows someone else who is about to!

AD-CHASING

How does ad-chasing differ from intro calling?
The procedure is basically the same, apart from the fact that you *know* that the company is recruiting.

You should make the client aware that you know that he/she is recruiting, otherwise you run the risk of them not actually admitting to this. Also, you will look very silly if you suddenly appear to know more than you did at the outset!

What to say
There are a number of ways to approach the client when calling. Here are some ideas of questions that you might try:

"I noticed your advert in the press/online recently, for an <role> and I am ringing to find out how that exercise is progressing"

"How successful was the advert in terms of volume and quality of response?"

"Out of curiosity, why did you decide to advertise directly yourself rather than use an organisation like ourselves?"

"At what point might you consider seeing more CVs as a comparison?"

Of course, there are many ways to phrase these questions.

ACTION POINT
Chat with your manager or other consultants to see what works best for them.

Think about what other things you might ask.

Additional points to make when calling

The goal of this call is to convince the client to either use you, or at least view some of your CVs as comparisons. Once you have convinced them to look at a CV, the next step, securing an interview for your candidate, is much easier.

REMEMBER
Recruiters are not always retained when they advertise for a client, even if they say they are! This means that there is no obligation for the client not to look at your candidates too.

Helpful points to make:

- Our candidates are a useful comparison – and there is no fee payable unless successful

- There is no fee for interviewing them

- Many of our candidates are exclusively registered with us, and won't respond to adverts directly

- We can introduce you to many candidates not actively looking at the advertised market

- Quality not quantity is important

- We do all the hard work in terms of pre-screening and monitoring responses when we advertise

- Direct adverts cost money regardless of success

If you have a great candidate, sell the benefits of seeing that candidate to the client. They will, after all, want to hire the best candidate they can.

IMPORTANT NOTE

The client you are calling will have had many calls like yours about the role.

Your style and tone are all important.

LEAD CHASING

Picking up leads is one of the most important parts of our role as a consultant.

Finding out who is recruiting is a great method to focus our BD. It is much easier and more efficient to build a map of the marketplace by talking to candidates about who is or has been recruiting, than spending hours cold calling businesses to discover the same information.

A simple question such as "Where have you interviewed or had your CV put forward to recently?" can provide such great market information, that you must ask it often.

Once a live lead is picked up, the process of chasing it is similar to making introduction calls and ad chasing, with some small differences.

Chasing a lead

Once again, it is really important that you make the client aware that you know that he or she is recruiting.

Start with a question like:

"I understand/believe that you may be currently recruiting, and I wondered what stage of the process you are at, and whether I may be able to help?"

Note that the client will undoubtedly want to know how you found out. You should be honest, but not too specific. A statement like "I heard on the grapevine" or "it's my job to know these things" will only make you look smug.

It is much better to say:

"A candidate of mine mentioned it to me during an interview" or, **"one of my clients mentioned that they had heard that you were recruiting, and I was really ringing to check that this was the case, and to see how I could help".**

If the client then asks for names, it is fine to tell them that due to client confidentiality, you hope that they understand that you are not able to say.

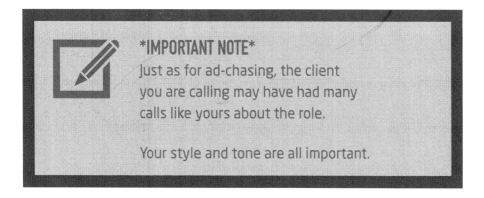

IMPORTANT NOTE
Just as for ad-chasing, the client you are calling may have had many calls like yours about the role.

Your style and tone are all important.

At this point your client **MAY** volunteer all the information, however, they may be reluctant to. Here are some potential reasons:

- They have engaged or spoken to other agents

- They have already seen CVs

- They have a preferred supplier agreement in place

- They are at final interview stage

- They have already offered or filled the job

Other information we need

Regardless of the situation, there is some important commercial information that we need to ask in order to start to build a relationship with the business for the next time.

- Are they aware of our business, and why didn't they contact us?

- How can we get involved now if we are not too late?

- How can we look to be involved next time?

- What is the best way to build a relationship with them for the future?

THINK TEMPS!
Whenever a client is recruiting, there is the
potential for a temporary solution.

Don't forget to ask the question, and sell the
benefits of temps.

A temporary solution is a great way to increase
revenues, and improve service levels too!

Going forward

It would be very useful to know who he or she has met already but
this information needs to be gained with some care. Explaining that if
you know the person in question, the client's thoughts about them will
help you to hone your efforts.

Regardless of the outcome of these conversations, you must always
leave an action plan, that **you** will undertake. This way you maintain
control, and have the client's permission to do so.

**REGARDLESS OF THE OUTCOME OF THESE
CONVERSATIONS, YOU MUST ALWAYS LEAVE AN
ACTION PLAN, THAT YOU WILL UNDERTAKE.**

CHAPTER 7 - CLIENT RELATIONSHIP BUILDING AND MANAGEMENT

Getting meetings and building relationships is a natural extension of the BD process, and one which can be a lot of fun.

In this chapter we will look at:

- Getting client meetings,

- Managing the meeting, and

- A simple sales or pitch formula.

THE CLIENT CYCLE

Just like candidates, clients also follow a life-cycle (shown in the diagram below).

This starts with our first contact with them, and moves through meetings, updating and keeping in touch, to taking a job brief, placing candidates and continuing the relationship on.

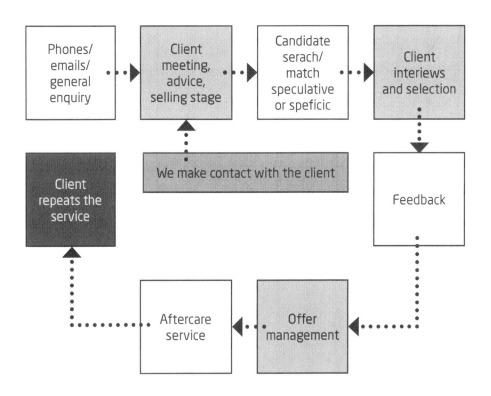

In this module we will look at the first part of the client cycle. Maintaining contact is dealt with in the BD module and everything to do with the job process is included in the next module.

Getting client meetings

Meeting clients is a vital part of our BD process. By meeting clients face-to-face we can build significantly stronger personal relationships than it is possible to do by phone alone.

We should aim to meet all our clients, whether they are large or small, provided that it is beneficial.

During the course of a phone call it is possible to assess whether a meeting would be beneficial to you, once a level of rapport has been established.

Clues that a meet will be beneficial include:

- The client has a live vacancy

- Someone else in their business has a live vacancy (if it's for someone else in your business, pass the phone over!)

- The client has recruited in the past 12 months

- The client will recruit again in the next 12 months

- The contact has a reasonable sized team

- The contact will be able to provide you with further valuable information about the company or introduce you to target contacts.

What to say
"Could I come to meet with you, perhaps half an hour one morning, in order to learn more about your business and start to build a long term relationship for the future?"

The benefits of meetings for us
There are numerous reasons why we would want to meet a client. Some of the benefits to you are:

- It differentiates us from our competitors and it is much easier to impress face to face

- It gives us a greater chance of gaining exclusivity in the future

- It allows for a more professional approach

- It enables us to improve our image with clients

- It helps generate new business

- It increases the chance of us filling a job, as we have greater control over the client

- It will engender a closer client relationship

- It gives us a greater chance of 'selling' advertising or a retainer

- It will enhance our knowledge of the company, which enables us to better brief our candidates

Practically, every client and every job warrants a meeting, but only if we identify this on initial contact, and if we believe that we are capable of convincing them and 'selling' the concept as the most sensible and beneficial solution to our clients problems/needs.

THINK TEMPS!

For temps, a meeting may not always be the best possible solution, particularly if the client has already briefed a number of agencies. Speed is the key for temps, and the phone is usually the best approach. You can always meet the client once the job is filled.

If you are meeting a client for a permanent job, take your temps colleague with you; they may be able to sell the client a temporary solution, in addition to the permanent solution!

To get a meeting to discuss a job

Always ensure that the client is left feeling that their need or requirement is unique and important. You may have filled many similar roles before but they mustn't be made to feel that it is just another standard order.

Key selling points include:

- Importance of the role and getting it right first time

- Gain a better understanding of the company culture and 'likely fit', which cannot effectively be achieved over the phone

- Enables us to give best advice on recommended approach and ultimately assists briefing candidates in a more effective manner.

To get a meeting on a general basis

Key selling points include:

- You will learn more about the organisation, structure and culture

- It benefits them in the long term, as we will be able to act quickly when they are recruiting

- It enables them to be able to relate to us and to gain information on current market conditions/salaries etc

- We are meeting a colleague in another part of the business or a client in the same location

- It's a natural next step following the call.

PREPARING FOR MEETINGS

Great news! You have got a client meeting booked. Now let's look at the meeting itself.

First things first – we need to look at getting prepared and building rapport.

Preparation

The more prepared you can be for any meeting the better. Today with information literally at our finger tips, there is no reason at all to 'wing it'.

Here is a simple check list to be sure that you are fully prepared:

- Check the address and contact details; remember that the database may be out of date, or the business may have multiple locations. Update your database as needed.

- Are you meeting the decision maker? Should you ask for any other relevant people to be at the meeting?

- Look into any background between your business and the client. Are there other consultants who can shed some light for you? This may not be on your database's notes.

- Check the company website, LinkedIn, Twitter, and any other relevant websites for information on the company/firm you are visiting and the people you are meeting.

- Plan your objectives – what are you looking to get from the meeting. What is your minimum and maximum objective?

- Do you have anything you should take with you? e.g. adverts file, mock up adverts, sample CVs?

- Is the person you are meeting a live or ex-candidate and is there any background you should know about or understand?

Meeting basics

- Be on time

- Look smart, alert and smile

- Remember reception etiquette – don't ignore anyone, the person watering the plants may well be the MD!

- Have your presentation, business cards etc all with you

- On walking from reception with the client or PA, establish easy rapport (discuss the weather, traffic, general news/business etc)

- Make sure you have a good handshake – if in doubt, practice with someone

- The first 30 seconds are vital, so make the right impression from the start

ACTION POINT

Talk to your manager about how they structure and prepare for client meetings

Do you have an information pack you should take with you?

Get a manager or more experienced consultant to come with you to meetings until you feel comfortable on your own.

RAPPORT AND CONTROL

Running a successful client meeting requires a subtle mix of rapport and control. As we know, people buy people, and they buy us before they buy from us.

It is important to start the meeting with a high level of rapport, and build up a level of control as the meeting progresses. You can see how this works in the diagram below. The level of rapport will reduce as it is replaced by control, but at the end of the meeting level of rapport will still remain.

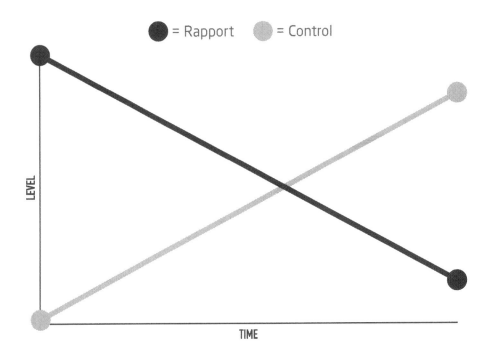

Rapport:

- Use the early part of the meeting to gauge what type of individual your client is, e.g. formal or relaxed, outgoing or reserved.

- Try to reflect the client's style in your delivery - remember **people buy people**

- Rapport needs to be balanced with control, which enables you to steer your client into giving you the result you want - to achieve your objectives.

Control Techniques

Controlling a meeting is essential if you are to achieve your objectives. However, as mentioned above, this must be balanced with rapport.

Here are some pointers to use and consider during a client meeting:

- At the start, **define, set, and get the client's agreement to the agenda**.

Try something like: **"In terms of this meeting today, I have a bit of an agenda in mind, if that's okay?"**

This introduces structure to the meeting, and gives the client your roadmap to follow.

- **Stick to the agenda**, however much the client wants to move the process on.

If they do move away from it, simply move back again and continue.

- Ask lots of **open questions** - never assume that you know the answer to questions that you haven't asked

- **Probe** into the answers you are given

- **Take notes** (but remember to keep as much eye contact as possible)

- **Use silence** - once you have asked a question, remain silent and wait for the answer.

The other person will always speak if you don't.

- **Listen carefully** and attentively. As the old saying goes, you have two ears and one mouth, use them in that proportion

Suggested agendas/structure

When meeting to discuss a specific job, use the agenda:

1. Company
2. Job
3. Person
4. Salary
5. Process

In a general meeting, this can be adapted to:

1. Company
2. Department
3. Typical requirements
4. Current relationships
5. The person you are meeting
6. The relationship going forward

FURTHER CONTROL TECHNIQUES

During the meeting you will want to hunt out and understand the things that are important to the person you are meeting.

Each individual will have a mix of business and personal needs that are important. Understanding these will allow us to relate our proposed service back to the client specifically, and highlight the impact on their business of success or failure in identifying the best solution.

Understanding the business and personal needs will help us to control, persuade and influence.

REMEMBER

People buy things, and especially expensive things when they perceive a need and value

Think back to the example in the BD module about a Casio Vs Rolex watch

If we understand what is important (what their needs are), we can structure a solution perfectly, that they will want

Some common potential needs to consider:

Business needs

- The need to find the exact blend of personality, experience and capability

- The right appointment will help the business develop

- The right appointment will help the company make more money

- The right appointment will bring about the change required in the department

- Getting it wrong will not achieve any of the above

Potential personal needs - Line Manager

- Do not like having to cover for vacancies (potentially working extended hours)

- Want to identify a potential successor to enable them to move on

- Want to expand their empire

- Do not want department morale to slip

- Want to limit workload in order to fulfill family commitments

- Might be under pressure from superiors to fill the role

- Hiring a great new person will make them look very good

Potential personal needs - Internal
Recruitment and HR Managers

- Want to be seen as successful/adding value

- Want to make their mark with a particular department/director

- Don't want to appear as though they
  don't know what they are doing

- Want control over how things are done

- Do not want to be excluded from the process

ACTION POINT
Discuss business and personal needs with your manager

Think about the impact of not achieving these needs and how you might use those in the process to persuade and influence

Closing a meeting

Once you have built rapport and gained an understanding of the various needs that are important, you will be in a good position to close.

For a job meeting

A simple method to do this is called SPIN. In essence, using this technique summarises the meeting back to the other person and offers a tailored (and if done well), obvious solution.

Spin stands for:

S   Situation
P   Problem/opportunity
I   Impact
N   Need = Solution

Using this closing technique has some significant advantages over other ways of closing a meeting:

- It checks and demonstrates your understanding and gets the client's agreement by summarising their needs back to them

- It enables the client to correct any areas where your understanding/perception may not be entirely accurate, and fill gaps if they feel you have missed something

- It creates empathy and a very positive feeling

For all meetings

Always finish the meeting on a positive note. This should include a call to action – e.g. what you will do next, when you will be in touch again, sending CVs, sending a proposal, booking adverts etc.

A SIMPLE SALES/PITCH FORMULA

Here is a very simple and effective sales formula that you can use at a pitch or meeting of any description, be it a client visit, a job briefing or a more formal pitch.

It will give you a starting point and structure to follow, and ensure that you don't fall into some of the most common sales traps!

Simple 5 Step Formula

1. Ask open questions

- Question anything that seems unclear, or badly defined

- Do not move on until you are confident of

    o   The individual's needs

    o   The individual's perception

    o   The individual's view and the foundation/reasons for it

2. Confirm your understanding

- Confirm your understanding of the situation, the individual's needs, and the key issues

- Go back to stage one if you can't confirm these

3. Propose your solution

- Propose your solution, clearly and in simple terms

- Demonstrate why it meets the individual's criteria and how it addresses the key issues

4. Ask for questions

- Check and ask for questions, comments and agreement

5. Deal with objections

- Deal with any objections that are raised

- These should be covered by referring back to why the solution meets the needs

- Remember that price is a buying signal not an objection

- Go back to stage four until agreement is reached

6. Confirm agreement

- Confirm your agreement and action plan

CHAPTER 8 - JOBS

Possibly the most exciting part of a consultant's role is filling jobs. After all, getting jobs and filling them with candidates is what recruitment is all about.

In this chapter we will look at the key areas of:

- Taking a job specification ('spec'),

- Writing adverts, and

- Selling jobs to candidates.

TAKING A JOB SPEC

Before we can really get going on filling jobs, we need to understand what it is that our client is looking for. It is vital that you get this right.

Asking the right questions here not only allows you to focus on finding the best candidate for the role, but also enables you to manage the expectations of your client, and effectively control the recruitment process.

First things first

Initially we first need to understand:

- The company name

- Who we are talking to (name and title) and their involvement in the recruitment process

- The job's location

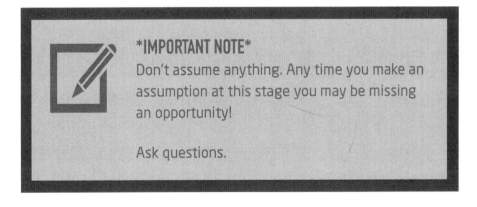

IMPORTANT NOTE
Don't assume anything. Any time you make an assumption at this stage you may be missing an opportunity!

Ask questions.

Are we the right person/division?

When a client phones, be sure that you are best person in your company to take the call. To do this you will need a little more detail, including their reason for calling.

If it is a job:

- The basic job title and job function

- The level of the role (experience or qualification required, executive, clerical etc)

- Whether it is a temporary or permanent role

At this point you will know if the call is something that you personally can deal with, or whether the call needs to be passed to another person, division or office.

THINK TEMP!
If the role is permanent there may be an opportunity to sell a temporary solution as well!

If we are still the right person/division
It's time for some fact finding. We need to ask about that person's experience of our business in the past (you can look this up on your database whilst you are speaking).

Then, find out what they have done so far. i.e. who have they called/ are about to call?

GAINING EXCLUSIVITY

Getting a job on exclusively is the ideal goal when taking a job spec. It means that we can work on the role unhindered by direct competition.

Why we want exclusivity

- Greater level of control

- Greater chance of filling the job/making the fee

- Closer working relationship with the client

- We have greater control of our time and are able to provide a better service

- Looks great to our candidates

- We can get a guaranteed return on our efforts

Common Objections

Selling exclusivity has many benefits, however you are likely to come up against some objections. The most common being:

- Need to spread the net as wide as possible

- Need to move quickly to see as many CVs as possible

- They have an excellent relationship with AN OTHER Recruitment Co, so want to give them a chance too

ACTION POINT

Think about these objections, and how you might counter them.

Discuss these with your manager or other consultants.

Notice how each can be turned around into a selling opportunity for you.

Ask the client what they will do if they receive the same CV from two agencies. Your response will follow on from how this is answered.

Gaining Exclusivity

To gain exclusivity, we must first establish the client's confidence in our ability to fill the job - without this you will never get exclusivity. Then you could use one or more of the following justifications:

- You have the best candidates and can provide a shortlist - there is no need to go elsewhere

- Reduces their time by not having to brief multiple agencies/ screen CVs etc

- A higher quality of service, and better candidates may get lost in volume of CVs sent

- You will take over the whole recruitment strategy ("one stop shop")

- Reduces duplication of effort/CVs/same candidates.

- Cost (can you provide a fee agreement in exchange for exclusivity?)

- Candidates will be fully briefed therefore definitely interested in this opportunity.

What if the Client has already gone elsewhere?
If the job is already out in the market, there are still a few things that you can do/suggest to the client to take a level of control.

- Make suggestions to gain time, e.g. provide a list of names of candidates from an initial search who will be covered by you.

- Ask who the candidates are that the client has already seen, so that we don't duplicate our efforts (this is also very valuable commercial information for you)

- Ask if the client wants you to talk to/pre-screen candidates first? If so, how will we avoid contacting the same candidates as competitors?

- Agree a solution, work through the scenario with the client remembering there is always a chance you can still gain exclusivity!

REMEMBER

We must always be very definite that we have the client's assurance that the position is and will remain exclusive.

This must be gained during the first telephone conversation - not subsequently or at a meeting etc (it may be too late by then!)

WRITING GREAT ADVERTS

Well written adverts are worth their weight in gold. Whether these are client paid media, or general online, they are a prime opportunity to beat the market to the best candidates who are actively looking. They are also an awesome chance to show the world who you are and who you represent.

Writing adverts doesn't need to be a chore, and if done well can give you that extra edge you are looking for over your competitors.

Top tips for writing great adverts

Here are our top tips to make sure that your adverts are head and shoulders above the everyday other stuff out there.

1. Focus on what you want to achieve

What do you want from the advert? The right response of course. So focus on the target audience and be sure to tell them all that they need to know to be persuaded to respond.

ponse you want

to fill this role only or are you looking for a general the marketplace? Do you want to put off unsuitable applicants, or would you like to see CVs from a wider variety? After all, those who may not yet be suitable for this role, may well be ideal for things in the future.

3. Start afresh

Doing what you did last time is not the way to go. A great advert written for another client may well have gotten a great response but this client is different, the role is different, and times are different.

Don't simply re-hash your last great work. Start with a fresh page, focus on this client and this role, now.

4. Be aware of your tone

Think clearly about who you are writing for. The tone of your advert must speak directly to your ideal audience, so adjust your tone accordingly. If in doubt avoid the overly salesy throw away comments like "Don't miss out" etc.

You are writing to individuals, so set the tone that way. Make it honest, attractive and specific to them.

5. Write as if you were speaking

Ad-copy doesn't have to adhere to all the niceties of perfect written English. It is more about tone, rhythm, simplicity and credibility. So, write as if you were talking to the person you want to attract and don't complicate your message. It's much easier to write clearly and punctuate properly if you do it this way.

6. Make it interesting - be creative

We know this is easier said than done, but you need to be original. Think about your client and the role, say something different that lifts you above the other adverts out there. Look for the USP of the role, and if you dig deep enough you will come up with something truly unique.

7. Be authentic

Authenticity is vital. Your target audience has heard all the clichés before. They are bored of over-sold roles, hyped up companies and unrealistic promises.

They want to hear the facts, told in an attractive, simple and realistic way. So sell them the real benefits, not just what you think they want to hear.

8. Put off the applicants you don't want

Remember you are ultimately being paid to get your client the right person, and where quality of response is important, you really need to deter those out there who apply to anything mildly interesting to them, and those who are just not right.

Using a screen in an advert not only improves the quality of your response, but also saves you time and effort weeding out the nos, the nevers and not in this life-timers, from the yes and maybe piles.

9. Proofread, proofread, proofread

There is nothing more embarrassing than pushing out an advert with an error in it. Check it, and then check it again. Then get someone else to check it for you. Be sure it is perfect before you press send.

10. One final thought

It's not just your target responders who are reading your advert. Your advert is also being read by your competitors, your clients, your future clients and your colleagues and bosses.

You are not only advertising your client's role and company, you are selling you. So, sell yourself in the best way you can!

SELLING JOBS TO CANDIDATES

Having interviewed the candidate, we now need to sell opportunities/ ideas to them so that we can send their CV to clients, organise interviews, take feedback and ideally handle the offer process.

Factors affecting your success in selling jobs to candidates

- Ensure you call at a convenient time (if calling a mobile, remember to ask if it's a good time for the person to speak)

- Establish key selling points of the job: Match selling points to motivations and extol virtues of the job. These should relate to what you know about the candidate from their interview and subsequent conversations.

  - o Role
  - o Salary
  - o Location
  - o Size/Profile of company
  - o Sector
  - o Career Progression
  - o Any others?

- Match the selling points of the role to the candidate's motivations, which you will know from the interview and subsequent conversations. Extol the virtues of the job.

REMEMBER

Your objective is to get permission to represent the candidate so that an interview can be arranged.

If the candidate is unsure, suggest that you try to organise an interview for them to find out more.

There is nothing to lose and everything to gain!

TOP TIPS

If an interview is offered and it is not possible to persuade the candidate to attend the interview, you could suggest an initial telephone conversation with the client.

It might be all they need to become interested.

The differences in selling temporary jobs to candidates

Generally the fundamentals are the same. However, speed is essential, therefore an exact match may not always be as appropriate, i.e. in-depth motivations etc. You are basically looking for someone who is available and can do the job.

The candidate is not necessarily seeking a long-term career move, i.e. money may be more important than job content for example. The client is usually only looking for a skills match, not a perfect personality fit.

The key selling points which apply to temporary candidates in relation to jobs

- Money

- Good company/well-known name on their CV

- Obtaining additional skills

- Length of assignment/commitment

- Any others?

CHAPTER 9 – MANAGING THE INTERVIEW AND OFFER PROCESS

O nce an interview has taken place it is really important that you understand the thoughts and motivations of both parties so that you can control and maintain as smooth a process as possible. As with most things in the world of recruitment, information is power.

In this chapter we will look at:

- Taking feedback,

- Offer management, and

- Handling buy-back.

TAKING FEEDBACK

Taking interview feedback is a really important part of the job process. It will assist us hugely in subsequent offer management (covered further in the next section) and will help us advise our clients as the best next courses of action.

Giving useful and accurate feedback is an area that consultants are often criticised for, especially where feedback is negative or following an unsuccessful meeting. It is never fun telling a candidate that they have not been offered a job they really want. You need to develop an honest but sensitive approach and this comes with thought and practice.

REMEMBER

There are two sides to the feedback process - the client and the candidate. Each is equally important.

Feedback is something that you should take time and care over. The questions you ask and the information you gain will help to manage expectations, and better control the process.

Why do we want feedback?

- We need to know if they have any reservations and what those are

- We need to know if they liked or did not like each other (and why)

- We need to know the level of their interest, and whether they are interested in continuing the process

TOP TIPS
The more questions we ask when getting
feedback, the greater our understanding
of each party's expectations following the
interview, and the easier it becomes to
anticipate problems and therefore facilitate
offer management.

Why do clients and candidates want feedback?

- To enable them to decide on the next course of action (if any)

- To enable them to improve their interview technique (if required - both client and candidate)

- To enable them to concentrate on positive or negative points if the process is to proceed

- To enable a client to pitch any potential offer at the right level

- To enable them to make any required changes in approach

THINK TEMPS!

In the temporary market, quick, concise feedback may be more appropriate since, if a candidate is not suitable, we need to immediately introduce others in order to influence the outcome of the assignment.

Typical questions to ask clients:

First interview:

- How did the interview go?

- What did you think of our candidate?

- How well do you feel they can do the job?

- How do they compare to other candidates you have seen?

- What reservations (if any) do you have?

- How many candidates are you intending to see?

- What is the next step?

For subsequent interviews:

- What is the person meeting them like as an individual/what is their background?

- What does he/she look for in an ideal candidate?

- What is the format of the next interview?

- Is there any specific preparation you would expect them to have done?

General:

- How happy are you with the quality of candidates you have seen?

- What can the candidate do to improve next time?

- If you have not seen anyone that is suitable, what will you do next?

- (Where negative) What was it about the candidate that you did not like?

Typical questions to ask candidates:

At all stages of the process:

- How did the interview go?

- How long were you there?

- Who did you meet? (this may be different from who you organised initially)

- What did you think of the people/person that you met?

- What did you think of the job and responsibilities?

- How did you feel you got on?

- What did you think of the company culture?

- How does it compare to others you have seen?

- What reservations (if any) do you have? (probe hard here, particularly if they say "None")

- What are your overall feelings?

- If you were offered the role at this stage what would you think?

- What other interviews do you have lined up?

OFFER MANAGEMENT

Offer management is not just something that happens once an offer is made. It is a process that begins at first contact with a candidate, and continues when first discussing an opportunity with them, through feedback, subsequent interviews, salary/package negotiation, to acceptance, resignation from current role and start.

It is the key part of the entire recruitment process when all your hard work on both candidates and clients is turned into actual fees.

Critical success factors

Being well-informed of positives and negatives throughout the process will reduce the number of times you are fighting to save desperate situations rather than enjoying smooth, confident and successful conclusions.

Things you must know (no surprises!)

Clients:

- Salary parameters.

- Benefits package.

- Start date required.

- Role being offered and its location.

Candidates:

- Salary expectation (and manage where necessary).

- Notice period and available start date (they might not be held to a long notice period, so ask if they will be held to their notice if longer than one month)

- Areas of concern/reservations.

- Current employer's likely response to their resignation. (This is important for handling buy-back, see next section)

Influencing a candidate acceptance

Being offered a new role is a big thing for any candidate. If we have managed the process well then an acceptance is the natural conclusion. However, sometimes we need to help a candidate with the decision to accept an offer.

Here are a few things to consider:

- Back up your arguments with FACTS! (Use your market knowledge to advise clients and candidates, putting the problem or concern in the context of the overall market place, quoting as many relevant examples as possible to reinforce your point of view.)

- Re-address the fit between the offer and the candidate's parameters and reasons for leaving their current employer.

- Ask them to talk to family and friends.

- Some candidates need time to make a decision. It could just be nerves about the move and the reality takes time to 'sink in'.

- Ensure smooth co-ordination with other consultants in your business. Once a candidate is 'under offer' they should not be offered more opportunities in most circumstances.

- Remember to congratulate them. Remind them how competitive the market is and how well they have done to get the offer (care must be taken, however, not to provide a false sense of security).

REMEMBER
You may handle an offer situation every day but remember it is critical to both clients and candidates.

Be personable, remain empathic and put yourse[l] in their shoes. Remember on a human level how stressful it can be for those involved.

TYPICAL OFFER MANAGEMENT PROBLEMS (AND THEIR SOLUTIONS)

There are a few typical problems that can arise during offer management. The more offers you handle, the easier you will find these to overcome, as well as pre-empt before they become problems.

Problems can arise in a number of areas, namely:

- **The job itself**

- **The client's personality**

- **The company itself**

- **The benefits package**

- **The role location**

- **Their current employer (Handling Buy-Back - next in this module)**

IMPORTANT NOTE
The more information that you gain through the interview process, and the better your feedback, the more easily you will have dealt with any of these even before an offer is made.

No matter how careful you are, there can still be issues. Candidates sometimes don't tell us everything. So, let's look at each of these individually and consider some solutions.

In connection with the job:

- Highlight any areas which are better than originally expressed when the candidate agreed their search parameters.

- Ask the client to flex the job spec, for example change some responsibilities or alter the emphasis of certain areas of work.

- Reinforce any new areas of challenge as an opportunity to develop experience. Reinforce any overlap of experience as an opportunity to project themselves as an expert rather than a beginner.

In connection with the client personality:

- Talk through the work background of the client and other members of staff in the department, management etc.

- Set up another meeting and brief the client (tactfully!) on the problem to be addressed.

- Consider an environment change for a further meeting - out of hours drinks?

In connection with the company:

- Name on the CV (big company).

- Opportunity to be more commercially involved (small company).

- Financial security (big company)

- No large company is totally secure, mention big company failures (small company).

- Prospects (big company)

In connection with benefits (additional to salary):

- Training (big company).

- More responsibility (small company).

- Broader overview (small company)

- Before giving the offer make sure you find out what the full benefits package is and what their financial worth is.

In connection with location:

- Find out about the area from the client or through other contacts and sell the benefits relevant to the candidate's aspirations.

- Review commuting patterns, different routes etc.

HANDLING BUY-BACK

Buy-back is the process of a candidate being made a counter-offer by their current employer to stay when they resign. This is a very common thing, and should be addressed during the feedback process, as discussed in an earlier section.

It is important to understand how the candidate believes his employer will handle a resignation and how they will respond.

You must get to the heart of this during your initial interview and subsequent discussions. It should be a natural conversation following on from their reasons for looking to move.

REMEMBER
Resigning from a role can be a stressful thing for many people and can involve a lot of mixed feelings (especially for more junior candidates who have not moved before).

You should always coach your candidate through a resignation, and help them remember all the positive reasons for moving on.

The reality of buy-back

When a candidate resigns from their role, it causes their employer a short term problem. The quickest and cheapest way for them to deal with that problem is to offer the candidate a pay rise.

If the candidate leaves they will usually need to recruit a replacement (involving recruitment fees) as well as handle any workload in the meantime if that replacement takes longer to start than the notice period in place.

Some points to make/consider when helping a candidate deal with buy-back.

- It is likely to be a response to a short-term personnel crisis and not a reflection on your future career prospects.

- Research shows that the majority of candidates who stay with their current employer under such circumstances come back within a year or less because their real reasons for leaving haven't changed.

- If your company recognised your work previously, then they would not need a threat like resigning to offer you a salary increase/new role etc.

- You may be marked as disloyal.

- The same things that were wrong with the job will still exist.- salary is only one item

- When your next review is due, you could be overlooked because you have already been given one.

- Staying with your company may be the easy way out, but is it what you really want?

ACTION POINT

Talk to your manager about buy-back and their experiences.

Think about how you might discuss buy-back with a candidate in advance of an offer to pre-empt a problem.

CHAPTER 10 – TIME AND PORTFOLIO MANAGEMENT

Achieving optimum efficiency as a consultant requires the right amount of time being spent on the right task. It is so easy as a new consultant to get pulled in many directions, and good time management habits built now will make a huge difference for you in the future.

In this chapter we will look at:

- How to manage your time,

- Some golden rules of time and portfolio management, and

- The outline of a perfect day.

GETTING THE MOST FROM YOUR DAY

Time is a major limiting factor in recruitment. To be really successful, you need to ensure that you spend appropriate amounts of time on the right tasks and that those tasks are done in the right order.

For example, there is no point spending half an hour during office hours discussing career planning strategies with an unplaceable candidate when you have a list of target calls to make. If you do want to speak to the candidate, arrange to call him/her later in the evening when your clients have gone home.

Good time management is all about planning and then effective execution of that plan.

Managing Time in Relation to Clients

However large or small your area (patch), and whatever level you are operating at, you will almost always find that 80% of your business is generated by 20% of your client base.

This is usually known as the **80/20 rule**.

The amount of time you allocate should also reflect this percentage.

When you start handling a portfolio of live jobs, often the first task that disappears from your daily routine is BD. If this happens revenue will also dry up as jobs get filled but there are no new jobs to replace them. This will lead to a very inconsistent pattern of revenue.

This is **not** the way to manage your business.

You should be looking for a healthy mix of job work and BD, to ensure a solid pipeline and steady revenue stream.

Time Management & Temps

The temps market differs slightly from the permanent market in that:

- There can be a requirement to deal with a higher volume of vacancies at the same time;

- You may need to react quickly, which can result in a daily plan going out of the window;

- You will need to manage time more effectively in order to continually maintain, and indeed develop, business.

You need to avoid becoming totally reactive rather than proactive.

Managing Time in Relation to Candidates
To start with you need to have an effective TNQ process, and only register those candidates whom you can help.

Then, when registered:

- Manage your candidates' expectations - agree suitable times for update calls etc.

- Prioritise hot (best) candidates.

- Sell exclusivity to candidates where the opportunity presents itself.

- Keep your database files and notes up to date and CVs ready to go.

- Try not to speak with candidates during office hours unless necessary (with the exception of temporary candidates, or if you are in a speed/CV race on a new role).

- Talk to candidates in the evening - they will be more relaxed and receptive, as they are unlikely to be interrupted by their boss.

- Identify a core of key candidates within your marketplace and ensure that you have interviewed them properly, or at least spoken to them in depth, and that you understand their needs/desires/motivations. This will speed the need to search regularly.

- Ideally keep in touch with candidates on an appropriate basis.

GOLDEN RULES

The Golden Rules of Time Management

For planning and prioritising, using a diary or work list is a great habit to get into. This might be manual or electronic, or a part of your database's functionality. Whatever format it is in, have one and use it religiously.

Then:

- Plan and prioritise tomorrow's activities as the last task of the evening before finishing for the day.

- Refer to your diary first thing in the morning, to remind yourself of what you are doing.

- Tasks/jobs which have a higher priority should be tackled first, rather than the easier ones.

- Never leave the 'nasty stuff' until last, particularly difficult phone calls. Get them over and done with so they don't prey on your mind and distract your concentration from the positive things that you need to do. *

- Break down large projects into manageable chunks of work. This keeps the boredom factor at bay and allows you to fit in other priorities as they arise around the project.

- Consider medium/long-term goals – personal and business objectives that you can work towards.

- Never use administration as an excuse to avoid the telephone – do calls first and leave administration until the end of the day.

- Never ignore action points in your diary or delete them because you don't want to do them. Only cross off tasks when you have completed them. You put them on your work list for a reason. If you do this you are only fooling yourself.

- Never put off until tomorrow things which you need to do today. Conversely, never do something today which can be put off until tomorrow if the task is standing in the way of bigger priorities.

* If this is a problem for you I can really recommend Brian Tracy's book 'Eat That Frog!'. Follow his advice and you will never look back.

The Golden Rules of Portfolio (Job) Management

Planning and prioritising should be a subset of your overall time management plan.

- On live jobs set time targets for shortlisting

- Keep an eye on and analyse your statistics - Number of CVs to Interview, 1st interview to 2nd, 2nd interview to Offer etc. The more relevant CVs you send, the more interviews you will get, leading in turn to more offers.

- Review newly registered candidates daily.

- Use technology sensibly to contact candidates about new jobs, but don't forget the personal touch.

- Sell candidates into clients prior to sending CVs (very relevant for a temp desk).

- Avoid too much searching of the database - know when to call it a day.

- Only shortlist candidates who are genuinely interested.

- Use your colleagues to refer/recommend candidates.

- Take and give feedback promptly

ACTION POINT

Talk to your manager about how they manage their time.

How does your office work - do consultants do the same things at the same times, or are they independent?

What are your targets, and how will you plan to achieve them?

A PERFECT DAY

Here is an outline of a sensible time management plan for your working day.

For this example I have divided time into Live time and Dead time. You might think of these as Client time and Admin.

Live time is client focused time. Dead time is when your clients aren't available to you and is the best time to do admin/interviewing tasks.

The Perfect Day Plan

08:30 to 10:00 — **DEAD**

Review today's plan

Emails

Review new registrations

Search jobs

Candidate interviews

Read relevant internet articles and news

Return urgent calls

Clear your in tray

Client visits/meetings

10:00 to 12:00 — **LIVE**

Call clients

Chase leads/ad chases

Follow up client's interview feedback

Chase shortlists/CVs sent

Organise interviews

12:00 to 14:00 — **DEAD**

Call candidates on jobs/feedback/offers

Search jobs picked up in the morning

Interview candidates

Lunch

14:00 to 17:00 — **LIVE**

Call clients

Chase leads/ad chases

Follow up client's interview feedback

Chase shortlists/CVs sent

Organise interviews

17:00 to close — **DEAD**

Call candidates on jobs/feedback/offers

Candidate update calls

Plan tomorrow

This is a good outline to follow and you may well think of many things that would fit into both live and dead time. e.g. writing adverts, updating the database, market mapping etc.

However, as much as possible, it is good practice to fit these into the right time.

When you should break these rules

- You get a hot candidate to work on

- Speed race on a new job/temp job

- Client meetings that can't be in dead time

- When its commercially silly not to - if a client calls and asks you to come to discuss a new role in the middle of the afternoon, you would.

SOME FINAL THOUGHTS

I hope that you have found this book useful and inspiring, and that the skills and lessons discussed help to make a real difference in your career.

If you keep an open mind and learn from every experience, with the right effort you will be very successful indeed. There is no other industry I know of where you really do get out of it what you put in. The more effort, the more reward.

Of course I'd love you to win every time but as with most things in life that just isn't possible and from time to time things will go wrong. When they do, just lift your head up, learn from any mistakes and move on.

Remember that doing the basics right will always produce great results in the long term.

The world of recruitment is a really wonderful place. Enjoy every minute of it.

SOME THANK YOUS

It is rare in your professional life that you are able to say a heartfelt and public thank you to those fantastic people who have helped you and made a real difference along the way.

Most importantly, I am lucky to be married to the most wonderful and understanding woman in the world. To my wife Mandy, thank you for absolutely everything – the highs, the lows and the in-betweens (and of course for all your hard work proofreading this book!).

To the colleagues and bosses I have worked with over the years. Many of you have been so much more influential than you will ever know. The teachings, help and guidance that you have given me will be with me always. In no order whatsoever, thank you Jamie Newman, Gary Watson, Kath Roberts, Renny Hayes, Steve Hockey, and Paul Kinsey.

NOTES:

NOTES:

....

....

....

....

....

....

....

....

....

....

NOTES:

Printed in Great Britain
by Amazon

66586036R00080